Unmade Hearts: My Sor Juana

July Westhale

Harbor Editions
Small Harbor Publishing

Unmade Hearts: My Sor Juana
Copyright © 2024 JULY WESTHALE

Cover art by Hillary McCullough, "futility of contentment"
Cover design by Brianna Chapman
Book layout by Allison Blevins and Hannah Martin
Author photo by Rachel Castillo

UNMADE HEARTS: MY SOR JUANA
JULY WESTHALE
ISBN 978-1-957248-17-2
Harbor Editions,
an imprint of Small Harbor Publishing

for Em

Introduction

Dearest reader,

Sor Juana Inés de la Cruz was renowned for her remarkable sonnets, among other writings, which pivot on the page in their original Spanish. They are tightly rhythmic and enact the content of their verse beautifully on their own; her love poems sing with playfulness and seduction on one page but rage and stone-cold grace on another. Her burlesque poems, of "the bedroom and the bullring," render her lovers both hero and saint (yet never God).

I began this project with the intention of ambitiously translating Sor Juana's sonnets with as much integrity as I could. When I was able, I adhered closely to the incantation-like qualities of Sor Juana's poems; however, I often abandoned the sonnet form for the sake of content.

You'll notice nothing in these pages resembles, even marginally, a sonnet. Upon completion of these translations, the global pandemic hit, a(nother) war in Europe started, and I simultaneously changed my entire life. It didn't seem like anything needed to, or should, follow a form anymore. I sat on these translations for four years.

One day, while reading fragments of Sappho, I had a thought—Sor Juana, who is already so widely translated, may not need yet another specific translation, nor another literary citizen thrusting retroactive taxonomies on her person. However, there is something about both the process of translation and the process of coming into wholeness within queer desire that is akin: the seams of both show. Meaning is made through iteration, then reiteration. Through intimacy with and intimacy without (other bodies and people to translate them). Everything clicked together in an aerial and clever way: why not take these translations and *show the work?*

Here you'll find Sor Juana's poems interrupted by my own poems and marginalia. An iteration of the intimacy of both poetry (which is a place we find ourselves) and queerness (which is a place we find ourselves).

The term "unmade hearts" has been taken from its original *corazónes deshechos* in many ways by many translators—often to suit the theme of the poem. If a heartache is occurring (and it often is, especially in her sonnets and burlesque poems), a *corazón deshecho* could be a *shattered* heart, a *destructed* heart, a *devastated* heart. It wasn't translated literally. As translators, we often avoid extremely literal translation, as it's not the most nuanced way of reading the emotions or context of a piece. However, in this case, I made a conscious decision to keep the unmade hearts literal.

Of the poems I translated (*Love Poems, Burlesque Poems*, and *Lamentations*), the construction of the heart is made wholly clear through Sor Juana's deft and daring ability to get inside of love, grief, sadness, expectation, desire, and push boundaries completely. She not only shows us exactly *how* a heart can be unmade, she shows us how it was made in the first place. And why.

I also chose not to include translations of her devotedly religious work in this collection. That may be a project for another time. For although they are stunning, worshipful, and ascetic in the cool, beautiful linearity she excelled at, I wanted to create a prism out of the deep desire, drive, and tumult that her work and legacy motions to on an individual level. Sor Juana was a woman of the cloth; this more richly informs us when we read the writings she dedicated to Earth-bound, mortal people. While we cannot entirely know what it was like to occupy her exceptional brain on an emotional level, she seemed to be the rare sort who wasn't burdened with religious guilt.

Because of her intense female friendships and her burlesque poems (erotic poems) addressed to women, Sor Juana is often posthumously identified as bisexual and held up as a queer icon in LGBTQ+ communities and scholarship. Together with her feminist writings and disinclination towards marriage, the nun's identity and presentation through her art made her a controversial figure, both during her lifetime and after. While there is no record that indicates how Sor Juana identified, her love poems are addressed to both men and women, and her subject matter challenges gender roles, the assignations of femininity and masculinity alike, showing forward-thinking and progressiveness during a very conservative 17th century.

We kill small darlings in translations; it's a heartbreaking endeavor. I'd argue that to translate is to simultaneously break the heart of yourself, the poet whose work you're inside of, and the audience. The monumental task of translation is not so much curating cultural nuance, language, song, and context–though that's vitally important. It is largely living with the fact that you will inevitably fail and will do so happily. The secret thanks you receive is being allowed to live in the borderlands between two languages and their resulting contexts and implications. It's a lucid state, a consuming one. A curatorial one. Your public thanks is being able to bring an artist you admire greatly to your own dinner table. I hope you will sit and feast with us.

Sor Juana's poems are extraordinary in their negative capability, especially considering her station as a woman of the cloth. Her words are bee sting and bee honey. I'd have been thrilled and terrified to have been an object of her worship.

I hope you enjoy, in good and poor faith.
With admiration,
July Westhale

Unmade Hearts:
My Sor Juana

SJ

Teach me love's only job is reason and convenience.

JW

& in duress & in faith & in lust
I reach for these wet pages—
and the least palpable of all abstractions:
logic. Or a gesture towards logic.

SJ

Every mortal being worshiped
is an ambitious beauty, with their alters
of idlers. Not full victims, themselves,
but idolizing victims, themselves.

As such, they only want their own,
and live in unfathomable fortune,
because they think—what more could be
as beautiful as a beggar's deceit, the construction of me?

JW

So, then, are we talking through the thin veil
of the afterlife? Your spine cracks, I have written
no no no & *o god yes*
and *no dejas de comer por comer.*

SJ

I am in measured recline, my attention
shaking. I only wish to report back, to observe,
to correspond in the pacing of letters—

but my yielding love is costly, salted
with the pleasure of being wanted—wanting
what is missing and what is not.

JW

Reason: I love you, and because of this
I am compelled to kill spruce,
pine, hemlock, and larch. Because
my nun parched her parchment,
her body inscribed. Because she made metaphors
of the bullring, and I disabuse them
of linearity.

Convenience? Because of this,
the ministry of *easy* is . . . what is
the word? There are palabras
and there are sin palabras, is this
a time to shake awake Hamlet?
Say, *what is between heaven and earth?* Be brave.

The word, though. What is it? Shoot
the moon? Do nuns play Spades?

Nil, I say. Be done with it.

SJ

If only my intentions helped bring the impossible
to light, a pain-poured cry of an unstable, undone
heart. Enough of these rigors, god, enough.

You aren't tormented by iron-handed jealousy,
nor suspicion (vile), nor quietude (contrasting),
with foolish shadows, with vain signs
that in fluent humor you have touched
and seen (on face, in movements)—
my unmade heart in your hands.

JW

O, salt me, O
salt me
salt me O

JW

[on nights when you clench my hip like a bear trap in your sleep]

with teeth expectant   I was once
cowed by quarrying animals   as a rule
I forbid fear   to rule me, often
the abstract gets in   and makes pedestrian
zoos of shared slumber   often
we live long enough to   see those rusted tusks wreck
our hips   with consistency
I have been afraid   exceedingly, now
my quaking denatures   alongside a brightness
in my chest   the place, they say, we hoard
rules and rules' embellishments   like a bear
or the idea of a bear   like a heart
or a proxy   I said it: I want
for want,   want for foulness and humdrum
as a rule   I disallow myself
control   on nights when your perfect
half-asleep   solitary   night-licked palm
reaches for the curve of me   curved not
like a comma   but like a psalm   I know enough
to know how very entrapped   I am not

SJ

The stories are unequal, yes, together
they exhaust us with extremes. To confess
is to be wanted, to be given freely.

JW

Translation, please.

We are the sort
of tired that adds extra vowels,
that does not deminutize.

Still, soldier on. Boats against the current.
Or is that only available to select few,
and the rest must have their contexts
exhumed by horny poets
many years after their own expiration?

What will become of me.

Poetry makes _____ happen.
Insanity is _____
and expecting the same _____.

SJ

A grievous love has lamented me.
This love saw death come closer, procured
that which was most raised—the fun soul
contains everything bad.

My aching adds pain to pain. And in each
considered circumstance it is necessary to die
one thousand deaths. When one
crashes and one turns, the exhausted heart
sends that sad ache home, home to a last breath.

I do not know what prodigious fate
returned to my memory and said
What do I adore in you? Who, in love, is most extolled?

JW

When I say *you*, am I speaking
to the fun soul gone home?
Or to the lover to whom I translate
all rigors of breath? It is not
for me to give voice to.

I am (only) a linguist. I cut my tongue
on the pride of one's vowels, and one's
other, sharper tongue.

SJ

It is not just a craving, to be hungry,
have hunger, or a whim,
to give love to my good, good one.
Not a soul could alight
your knowing. Not a soul
could deny, you deserve to be cherished.

.

JW

What, then
is love, and what is worth
writing about? Shall I invoke
your tender ear, or is it
the man who sees a crash
then vacuums the glass in his flowers?

SJ

And if my understanding of the wretched,
so incapable of knowing as they are,
is such a rude error even I could not find
forgiveness for my brazen ignorance—

then somewhere in heaven, someone heavenly
has known you, or has given you yearning
or taken your confession of sin, has suffocated
the genius of understanding.

JW

Today, two strangers in Prospect Park yelled hello in Farsi to one another. How much easier for them to say, "Hello, you are like me."

(My sweet one says: "Althusser calls that *interpellation*. He also killed his wife.")

The woman at the Quik Mart, curling her bangs at the register. Hoping.

Is there anything in your pages about this? Open at will—

SJ

Painless love scares the body.

I cannot leave you, nor have you,
nor do I tightly grasp the ardor
that makes a body search for itself.
That flawed pilgrim. Forget you? No. No.

——-

God died wanting us, pronouncing
his body, cursing us, holding power, court—
we will not utter, unrighteous, again.

JW

Why won't you answer me?
Am I writing my own death?

Hello?

JW

In sleep I dreamed a big and stuttering dream—two thousand miles between us, but the same finger-bones of clouds, like clots of blood after a fresh scrape.

Woke to the shaking and quivering of my cold winter windows, the empty pillow. An atomic bomb. In my last fifteen minutes, do I call those I love, or do I rest up for the after life?

I reach for the sky to hit snooze on this world. In sleep, my fist blanks out the moon.

A plane saunters forward, barren of bombs.

You're wrong in this. I am unafraid of painless love.

SJ

Which half of my heart does not want it all?
When I am resplendent in afterlife, all of it will
know I am the making, the unmaking.

Is this 17th century Mexican nun rly sliding into my DMs rn?

SJ

When my ungratefulness abandons me, I search
for it like a lover. I search for a lover, too,
one that pursues. I leave them, thankless.
I adore whom my adoration mistreats.

SJ

~~I mistreat those whom my love beckons.~~

JW

I'm sorry for making you sound
like a stammering greeting card.

SJ

In the dealings of ardor, I find diamonds,
and I am diamonds.

JW

Note in margins: for all dealers
of me want to know how I can be squeezed
to brilliance.

SJ

I live to see what kills me. I kill whomever wants
to see me beaten. For this I pay, I suffer my desire.
If I beg, I anger my boiling pride. There is no way.

But I, for the most part, pick a violent job,
one I want not. The one who does not want
me, who is looting me. Who is vile loot.

JW

For this reason, I have never liked diamonds
insofar as we have punished them into diamonds.

SJ

Resolving the question of which is more bothersome in
letters: the loved or the abhorred?

One is less terrible, though not more mollifying.

Both teach suffering, which cannot
survive without vain ignorance, which
sounds sweet to the ear. Like bone-weary moans.

JW

We come when language cannot.
Is it *dying a little death* or is it
moaning from the bones outward?

JW

Is it me you thirst for or you
reflected in me? Who wants
placidity? Who wants to reach
for the placid waters of others,
knowing it may about-face
and turn to the amnesia of snow?

SJ

Love, without my resistance,
makes a fire in an unmade heart.
It makes the chest's blood evaporate,
gone, before the eyes. My eyes

look downward in your presence, they know
you playfully, your sweet charm. My body
and self revere you—your visible rays

between all the dark.

JW

How they find the snowy
thickness, the resistance to light—
that which left as a vapor returns as a cry.

JW

My body, when it tastes,
tastes like wisdom because it is.

The ignorant say it is the very best of all worlds, less *bad* than
theory.

SJ

You know me, or you do not.
If so, tell me my sins so I might know.
If not, you have diminished understanding.

If so, we again remain unequal.
For how could you assure me of love,
loving tales of the impoverished mind?

Is there any decency in the fantasy of love??

The cursor blinks and blinks, a dull and loveless eye.

SJ

My requital is present. My torment is both
active and passive. I suffer, profoundly,
both in loving and in being loved.

SJ

Stop, shadow! O, evasive bounty, most wanted
spell. I've died content for pretty images. I've lived
tortuously with fictitious grace. It is a magnet
that serves the obedient steel of my breast.
Why court me with flattery if you plan to evade,
future fugitive? Why move to boast that you cannot
satisfy my triumph, my clandestine self—the tight bow
of your fantastic, clinging form? If you labor
in my prison's fantasy, no one pays attention
to whose arms you escape from, whose chest.

JW

I've died *content* for pretty images.
I've died. Content.
Pretty images.
What a way to say
we made all this shit up.

SJ

I contemplate my mercurial love:
how grave, the malice of my sin,
how violent, the force of desire.

In this same memory, I almost believe
my caution could cap the last line
of depreciation, the last terms of my employment.

I would want it *so*. When I reach your face
and you see my infamous ardor, you'd deny me.
Later, the just cause would avoid me, too—

JW

Translation note: I added italics to the *so*.
Weaponized immediacy.

SJ

—that can only be remedied in publishing it:
the grand delight of my wanting you
is only painful in the confession of it.

JW

Let's talk, shall we, about *aftermath*.
Is it all really so tidy? My own
threadbare self, and your pages,
would have me believe in holy mess.

SJ

What iron infamy goes the iron scorpion,
whose footprints filthily stain the floor.

JW

The you, how it shape-shifts.
Filth as common denominator,
filth as the only *sure thing*.

SJ

You cannot help but be deadly venom,
that harms and spills without warning.

JW

I see. So we are opening our libraries,
are we? What wisdom
in the tipping point between
adoration and abhorrence.
Even the holy fall prey to their own
internal weather. The same cheek
that was blurred with a nocturne's softness
cuts indiscriminately in mourning light.

SJ

In the end, you are so terrible and perfidious
you fail even at being abhorred!

And offered is your vile self, to my memory—
Fearful, I contradict it, though plead:
give me the pain I so deserve.

I consider myself: I've hated you. I've loved you.

Does your beauty want my boldness,
is your beauty sacred, and how was it
conceived? Is it a fearful dark
or one where the speaker falls
and wakes and falls, always continuing
the same dream, the same cast
and soundtrack? Do you want
my boldness, my hope?
Am I in your good employ
and just a poor employee of myself?

SJ

Am I in your good employ
and just a poor employee of myself?

SJ

No one wants to be forgotten or neglected.

My thoughts are distinct,
they are unable to forget you.
As if consigned to oblivion.
At least they do not understand how sorry they are.

To be capable of being loved is to be
capable of being forgotten; that is glory.
The potential to have *been*.

There is something less than victory, and it costs me nothing:
rather than forgetting—memory's compromises.

JW

Is hyperbole more ingenious than truth?
Do we aggravate ourselves with desire?
Do we willingly put miles
and husbands between ourselves and god?

You and your forgetting!

SJ

Go on. Deny that I have the capability to be
loved. Concede this glory, which goes
against your long-held position.

To attain this victory, you agree to forget
forgetting. You do not negotiate your memory.

SJ

The painful effects of love do not equal their steep price.

JW

Economics is, after all,
the study of social systems—the unmade heart
is economy?

SJ

See me following without a soul, a blunder
I too condemn as strange? See the blood
I spill on this and all other paths,

following the traces of a deceptive trick?
Are you so admired? Well, do you see?

More merciful than you is the cause of my pain.

JW

Notes in margins:
~~more forgiving than you is the cause of my pain?~~
~~Forgiving you is?~~
~~Pain is merciful where you are not?~~
Pain is more forgiving than love?

JW

Is the heart unmade like a bed, or like the spine
of a cactus, which is a modified leaf? Is it unmade
like a rerouted subway line, or like an afternoon
stuffed with too many orgasms? Is an unmade heart,
after all of this, the wet spot in the sheets?

Who will sleep there?

SJ

Suspicion of hidden cruelty, and the relief that hope brings.

Hope is a daytime affliction.
It entertains my tired years,
the faith in both good and harm alike
and the balance and equilibrium of the two.

What is always suspended, in tardiness
to incline oneself one way or the other,
is not the abandonment of deceit entirely—
deceit which arrives exceptionally large

in confidence and desperation.

JW

Here's what I got from that: whose name
have you quit? What homicide? You are most severe!
O, how. O, how. O, how I love you.
One avoids what is suspended in the sated soul.

Between ill-fate and the goodness of luck,
will you do nothing to conserve life
without fully dilating death?

Am I close?

How to counsel the zealous, epiloguing a series of loves.

SJ

Love commences in ravenous want,
with solicitations, adoration, and efforts.
Soon, it grows fat with risk,
sustained on the wails of suspicion.

Doctor it love with warmth and indifference,
that which is between deceit and flame.
Light the fire with the tears of fire.

JW

Love's beginning, its middle, its end, is this;
So why do you mourn the detour? This is all the same road.

What reason is there to be pained by this?
Love did not deceive you—
It simply ended, precisely on time.

SJ

Absence is an older wound than zeal.

The absent, the jealous—these are provoked
with far-away ire: presume
this absence looks not around to see
and feels far from the reality it touches.

JW

This template, perhaps, of crazy fury,
is one where discourse favors delirium:
without intermission of breath, of pause,
nothing reduces the force of suffering.

The doubtless upset of patience
certainly suffers upset—

SJ

—certainly pain opposes resistance.

Without resistance, sufferers remain unconsoled,
and if it is the pain of harm rendered, in the end,
absence truly is the biggest torment over jealousy.

SJ

In vain we reduce the grief of a jealous man to rationale.

Where is sanity? Where did it go?
To overcome tremendous zeal, one must
have furious extremes, marvelous
demonstrations of insanity.

What of you has so offended love?
Or why, in faulty love of all deceitful,
one is not assured of a powerful anything,
least of all the eternal possession of beauty?

—

With that, I accuse you of error/ignorance.
Fortune and love are the stuff of tales,
the propriety of which has not been given, without use.

JW

Possession is for temporary things.
Temporality is true, and it is abusive
to want to conserve them forever as equals.

SJ

I do not doubt that I love you,
though you've aggrieved me. Even more
that I am both the lover and the scorned;
the affection I receive is not that which I prefer.

I hold both adoration and detestation, and infer
that neither can be to such a large degree.
Still, I lack the power to have won hatred
without first having lost love.

If you think my soul wants you
due to your anemic affections,
I advise your vain self-satisfaction this:

if love has given entrance to hatred,
the lowest denominator is remiss.
The remiss will, in time, become nothing.

JW

Why solve for x if x is a zero-sum game

Note from margins: "For the five poems that follow, they've given themselves to poetic form, as well as the forced consonants of which they are made, a domestic solace."

—Sor Juana

Note from margins of margins: Did you really write so many poems to the wives of important men? Here they are. Here they are, and they unmake every person who has ever been a *wife*.

—July Westhale

SJ

I.

When they label you a scoundrel
and implore you to beg pardon for your ailments,
use the knowledge you have gotten from them:
how to cover the stench of fecal matter, before it poisons.

If you take the bait, there is no solo magpie
to blame for a bad year.
Let a flock of them fly;
all the world will be deafened with metaphor.

Let the blunderbuss make a racket of everything,
an emblem of all that's an emblem—
what's more, Ines, you're an old catch now

who knows well that my love is a sin;
I'm not tricked by your affection,
though you be a shank of meat, and I am holy.

II.

Although you are such a *lady*
you could unmake all the poor of Camacho,
you're disguised with shako
and a face painted without blemish.

Of the jobs your love dispatches,
one holds the sad cargo of a *macho,*
so overgrown and hard to penetrate
one cannot enter without crouching.

This makes a mockery of us and them,
and them from whom we are made,
what our own bellies have spit out:

the wisdom to understand when they suspect
what you have done, and I have done—
made love a foreign thing, sowing an unfamiliar crop.

I looked up *blunderbuss* and it is perfect and it is decided:
the unmade heart is a gun with a flared mouth,
shot at a short range.

SJ

III.

With your love I find myself—
and I confess that seeing makes me
want to gloat. Your beauty has remade me;
when you are jealous, I reveal myself.

If you look at another, I am annihilated.
I tremble with your grace and swaying
because I know your dance would not break
the mood, even for a bit of sustenance.

When you're angry, I do not pant.
When you make me itch, I hold strong.
When you leave the house, I do not repose.

I hope between this and that,
your love and my wine will meet me
in both the bedroom and the bullring.

JW

Jesus lord. The pen fails.
The bullring stammers wetly open.

SJ

IV.

Go with God. He is the lie that knows you even in stench.

Still, it is not reason enough to be your servant,
offering you other tastes of the carafe.

JW

As veiled as queer desire could be—instead
of "hello" in Farsi between strangers:
I offer you other tastes of the carafe.

SJ

You passed over your visage in the basin,
and my anger, when I am most the fool.
Be warned I will open
both our heads over such insolence.

Tell me, is it fine others defraud you?
And when, by your love, I turn off the lights
and you leave with that good-for-nothing?

I'll go with my story, and suffer
the cattle-prod of my mockery—
a, e, i, o, u.

SJ

V.

Although you presume me crude,
you also presume, as a moth, I am scorched
by your light. I assure you I am not—
having already recognized it as false.

Though I am tangled in your web,
scant little comes to dazzle me.
When it comes to color, I am an eye-rod
in sullen, dimmed quarters.

I do not itch for your touch.
Before, I was with others so fresh
I could have served you new ice.

Giving you my snow softens me,
and as such, you do not disappoint.
I know very well what I fish for.

SJ

I go with the God
you can only pretend to reach—
at the end of my long life,
an eternal rest.

Enjoy he whose birth
is the very start of fiery glory.
I wish only to unite
you with your own.

JW

They call you the *immortal sound & the fury*
and o, boy. What luck.

Luck, in Spanish, is *had*. Instruments
are *touched*. Ice cream is *taken*.

Such visceral and obliterating eros,
the joys of furious sound. Of a tongue
strategically pushing cold cream
from one shape to another. Is it any wonder

Victorians spoke in flowers, G. Stein coded
in buttons, and nuns, driven sharply dizzy
with want of another man's wife, pointed
to the carafe and said, *let me show you*
how the taste of something daily
and pedestrian—how, how, how
it is the opposite of signifying *nothing*.

JW

Love may not be reason and convenience.
Love may be psalms and lamentations.

SJ

Now I am alone
and my banishment
by grief or by relief
allows love to remain;

Now, stolen, I am
a brief amusement
for so many
impertinent eyes,

and, leaving their chests,
out come the ardent tears
of my cruel anxieties
and their repressed woundings.

Outside ceremonies
of courteous attention
show affected relief,
apparent consolation.

The mother's pain is outed,
breaking the radial bridge
of my tears, the rapid
torrent of my tears.

In exhaled beams of light
come confused sighs—
an embrace of weeping
that floods, that drowns me.

My heart spills over
pure, running blood
like the constant
fountains of my eyes.
There are many voices
of my pain, fogging
virgin mirrors
of the celestial sphere.

Suffering is published
through the torment
of most unforgiving
ropes and bindings.

Cede love to justice
and with extremes show
that only my heart
is a stable president.

In the end, my husband
died! How indignantly
I pronounce his death
without announcing mine.

Him without life, and me
alive in this weak state?
Me, with voice, and him deceased!
Me living, while he decomposes?

It is not possible; without a doubt
my treacherous love
and my profound sorrow deceive,
or life has lied to me.

If he was my soul and life,
how can I be alive
without a soul?
Animate, without life's force?

Who conserves my life,
and from where do they come?
What is this air that breathes,
this heat that foments?

Without a doubt, it is the love
in my chest that ignites
signals in me,
that show I am still living.

I am like the wood
that passionately loves the flame;
the same light sustains us
as the light we endure,

and when the compostable
humor in it perishes,
it seems we live
and not that we must die too.

So I, in the mortal
cravings of my soul,
find encouragement
in the sorrows of eventual death.

O, of a time that ends,
and is not cowardly
for resisting death
so many times!

O, how the transparent
sphere falls around my feet
and poles are built up
on adamantine axis!

O, the center in its cavern
lends me shelter
covering my misfortune
with Earth's machine!

O, the sea between waves
forces my surrender
in misery, to feed
its voracious fish!

The sun denies my eyes
its brilliant rays,
and the air of my sighs
their necessary climate!

Cover me, eternal night,
and always darken my heart.
Erase my ill-fated name
from the chests of the people!

O, God! That all
cruel creatures should
want to live because
they like the pain of it!

What do I wait for? My own
pains take vengeance on me.
My throat serves
only funeral chords.

Says the example of me,
to a wounded all:
here a life lay sleeping
because a love once lived.

JW

A long-distance relationship
must make do with pretty images:
pretty one thousand miles, and one
thousand more. Is pretty pretty
alone in separate cities,
or is it only lonesome
in the forest killed to print its pages?

SJ

This is not to praise you.
What does applaud you
would make hoarse
the bleating of bugles.

He who copies
the sun, although more
beautifully, will never
achieve all the sun offers.

JW

The more intense
the study, the more
beautiful the rendering—
yet, still. Only a painting.

I will not waste away in the attic of another.

SJ

If you wish to be
applauded, praised,
do not make of yourself
a cheap copy. A lie.

JW

How did you get away with this & to a wife?

SJ

Live. At your age,
the sun that assists you
will never measure up,
only illuminate you further.

JW

Who among us has not called
those whose names are in our mouths
the sun or the sun's proxy? You say
live, as if it's simple.

SJ

Live in fortune,
in placid consortium
with your sweet husband
and your steady lover.

Like the exalted sow,
whose royal lineage
unites her glorious
bells of praise.

A good many heroes rescue
through devoted memory.
Memory lives because I,
in your light, live there too.
I only live there
because I believe you do.

SJ

Because I cannot
throw myself at your
feet (because fortune
does oppose my very wish),

I am the very embers of faith,
the very sign of the faithful—
my heart owes you
your imperiousness.

Enviously, I give these wishes,
badly formed in verse,
in which the only mercy
is that they are truthful.

I do not wish to say, but will:
I ask the heavens
not that you endure eternity,
nor survive the centuries through—

these modern courtesans
are in the fashion of flattery,
and are from the palaces,
not from the convents—

Nor do I wish you my luck,
which I have for certain:
to love the world is achievement
enough, and perpetual.

JW

The Brooklyn world outside glass
as thin as membrane: one direction
holds the waves of Coney Island
like a bright blue maw. The other,
the bomb-like planes of JFK,
which wake me from the astral plane
where my love and I
share the same wet sheets.

Startle me, O openness, into next level
knowing the origins of pain and pine alike.

SJ

Pain does not automatically
mean achievement, a prize!

JW

Here I take my daily page, the hymnals
of those who came before but did not
throw themselves publicly at the feet
of all our greatest and brightest balls of gas—

SJ

No, sir, that is miserable.
Misery in desire
always asks for more,
and solicits even less.

SJ

I approach and abandon
myself: who if not me
can find absence in eyes
and presence in the cast-off?

JW

Woe to those for whom
contempt is still a lost path!

SJ

So attentively I adore her
that in my suffering
I do not suffer her rigors
as much as I miss them.

I see in my destiny
the precision of my banishment.
I despised myself more
because I lost less.

JW

O, who taught you?
Whoever did so did so
exquisitely & halfway: banning
the despised brings love.
God, no.

SJ

I live, ignored, in your light.
I abandon myself
where not even my sins
are as disdainful as my gifts.

JW

Should we have oatmeal first or oral sex?

SJ

The sad fantasies of an absent heaven—

JW

O, STFU!

SJ

Loosen the tightened
string. I fear you'll
burst if you turn, then
turn around again.

JW

Memory, when it is tidy,
allows, for just a moment,
calms any persistent sorrow.

SJ

If you cease my sadness with your awful tyrannies, do you
end my life?

JW

I am not so rude
as to think that life
is only worth living for the loved.

SJ

Truce is a form of torment.

You well know, like one
close to heart, only
how to estimate, to mimic
a feeling of closeness,
and because the one
close to heart was lost,
loss becomes a strength
that demands eternal durability.

JW

In this, I ask
for clemency. Not
because I live,
but because you do not die.

SJ

Is it not enough
to have committed to memory
the tender caresses, the sweet
words, the noble finery?

JW

I think not.

SJ

And is it not enough
that industriousness grows
from past glories
and my present sorrows?

JW

Is it not enough
to be enough?

SJ

Woe to me, my
goodness! Who could not
give you this grievance,
and not fear my offense!

JW

There are those among us
who would have our grief stay,
who would say it is impossible—there aortas of the heart
are thusly ecstasy and death—

SJ

Form it, with foolish sharpness
and strung words,

answered actions, and their propositions,
interpreted for me by you.

JW

The very job description of *translator*—

SJ

On this, in peace,
I serve a war.

JW

Why do you test
all you meet? For chance
we may deserve your lovely
eye, your tender attention?

SJ

Is there another beauty
that perchance warrants
higher merits, touches
sweeter than those before?

JW

You got it so bad.

SJ

Why do you vet
with superfluous questions?
Is not *moving*
the daughter of *absence*?

I already know
of nature's fragility,
and that her consistency
is in not having her.

I know that movements
happen in periods.
In them, one's
expired ailments live.

Yet I also know
there has been rigidity
and exceptions
to the common law.

You want, only for you,
for all to be possible.
Why of that,
and yet not of this?

But, ay! I hear
your given answers,
on the safer side
of adversity.

This confusing war
strikes fear in me.
You have me suspended
between life and death.

Come over to someone's
party lines and agree:
allow them to live
or let them die in peace.

JW

You hardly went white
when the predatory archer
achieved unfailing success
with his shot,

when in my loving chest
bloomed the flames
of reciprocal fires
and keen confirmations.

SJ

Is it enough
how alive I am?
How I give my absent
heaven the divine cloth?

SJ

You haven't seen,
my love, when the iron world
softens its arms of gold,
the moon in a mirror

which reflects beautiful
rays in crystal, repercussive
wounds, and the closest,
most emulated object.

JW

The arrows
in my breast face
the resistant
snow of you,
their tips rounding.
Standing ovation.

SJ

Love—

JW

Translator's note in margins: divine, holy?

SJ

is only reason to reach
for other trophies.

Tell others of the ruins
of my undone valor,
which rises in contrite
ashes and predicts lessons.

My heart speaks it.
Eternal fathers stand
guard, inexhaustibly,
over the testimonies of fire.

JW

I hate how erased, how policed,
how gatekept—

From the bloody tacks,
ruined arrowheads spread
gentle poison
through an arch of veins.

SJ

The severed, disembodied
voices echo, and go on.
Love is propelled forward,
if only to retain respect.

My eyes are little girls.
They look backwards—

JW

Will you turn to a pillar of salt,
will you lose your Eurydice
for daring to share
the sun's jubilance with her?

SJ

—glance backwards, parlay
sincerity with a look,
a secrecy of souls.

The troubled countenance

JW

Translator's note in margins: *and the hindered breath*

SJ

in whose mute, calm
speech voices affection—

JW

Translator's note in margins:

To tell you more
is to explain less,
to desire denial
by knowing the map of it.

SJ

—my lynx-like mind
penetrates the most
hidden breasts.

I've said it true:
my love is assumed
to be correlative
of your merits.

JW

"The evident contexts
of my fineness" is such a flex

SJ

They will be sufficient
for you. I shall not
proceed, lest I offend
with yet another superfluous mouth.

JW

O my dear one, with the eyes
like little girls—do you not know by now
the mouth is never superfluous?

Had, touched, taken. The grammar
of conquest. The grammar of heaven.

SJ

Just in case the ashes
of my dead hope
become liberated
by some weak branch

where one can find oneself
with limited strength—
in the moment you listen
to me, my soul enlivens;

just in case the deadly
scissors threaten to cut
the small truce I have

JW

with death's face,

SJ

listen, in sad lamentations,
the tender consonants
brandish funeral rites
to a bevy of swans.

JW

A sad bouquet of courtship,
my book of swans.

SJ

And before the eternal light,
with its lethal, opaque key
closes for good
before my tremulous eyes.

JW

Something, something about gentleness
lancing through bodies, the union of souls—
in Spanish, *Celestial City* is *la más allá*

SJ

Your sweetness echoes in troubled chains.
No solace between words.

JW

A case for poetry: white space. Breath.

Is your face loving? Or is it made so
by mine, looking at it?

SJ

Your face bathes coldly
in the vigor of your weeping.

Your tears and mine.

Tell us we are mistaken.

That two hearts, in different chests,
engender the same cause.
Our hands are one, woven
palms saying
with movements
what lips have grown quiet.

Unmade heart: psalms.
Unmade heart: lamentation.
Is your faith, still, unviolated? In English, we choose a
more-flowered term: unbothered.

SJ

When I go down
to Styx, your faith
will be the coins
I use to rent the boat.

Take these lips,
fed with breath
from an inanimate chest—
inanimate from mortal anxiety.

JW

Translator's note in margins: inanimate or dead, and
mortal like dead or mortal like common?

SJ

The fevered spirit
can be called *valiant*
when in the act of serving
an organized earth.

JW
The breast contains this message.

The marooned heart,
the heavenly boss,
an eternity of my rare value.

JW

Goodbye to all that—

SJ

To love you is to stray from you.

SJ

Advice to my disappointment:

Hello, my disappointment.
Already you arrive
at the most extreme you can be
while staying true to yourself.

JW

I believe
even the cost of everything
is cheaper than the warning.

SJ

There is nothing to be jealous of
when it comes to flattering love:
it is a lesson very remote from risk.

Disappointment is an illness
that doesn't seek its own cure.

On the same path of the lost
are similar ailments:
if I've lost the treasure,
I've at the very least lost the fear.

Not fearing fear is a balm to me—
no terror for the thieves
nor their naked passengers
held captive against their wills.

Nor the same liberty
to have a thing because I want it so,
the desire itself is dangerous
for all I already possess.

I do not want more untruths.
My soul isn't hearty enough for them.

JW

Advice to my happiness:

happy like disembodiment,
pleasures like heavy as everything.

SJ

What a hard law absence lays!
Who will repeal it? If when I
do not want you to take me,
without taking me, with my dead
soul, myself a living cadaver?

It will be your charms
living solitarily in the heart's
prison, silently. If I guard them,
I am an indignant janitor,
a fragile refugee.

Positioned as such, I leave
for the ultimate valley.
I promise you my rendered love
and constant faith:
to love you always, to forget you never.

Author Biographies

Juana Inés de Asbaje, known as Sor Juana Inés de la Cruz, was a Mexican poet from San Miguel de Nepantla. She is considered by many to be the mother of Latin American feminism.

A great Baroque figure of letters, Sor Juana's work also constituted a certain artistic fashion that was far ahead of its time. Her knowledge and skill set were broad and included science, languages, writing, art, and philosophy. For her, poetry formed a part of cultural identity, and her verse displays a deep knowledge of musical history and poetic technique.

As a girl born out of wedlock from a family with little means, she was also entirely self-taught. Her birth certificate contains no census data, but her baptismal certificate indicates she was born around 1648. Because she displayed a gifted intellect at a young age, her parents sent her to live with family in Mexico City where she attracted the attention of the viceroy, Antonio Sebastián de Toledo, marquis de Mancera. He invited her to court as a lady-in-waiting in 1664. In 1667, given what she called her "total disinclination to marriage" and her wish "to have no fixed occupation which might curtail [her] freedom to study," Sor Juana began her life as a nun with a brief stay in the order of the Discalced Carmelites[1]. In 1669 she moved to the laxer Convent of Santa Paula of the Hieronymite order in Mexico City, and there she took her vows. Sor Juana remained cloistered in the Convent of Santa Paula for the rest of her life.

She died in 1695 of the plague.

[1] https://www.britannica.com/biography/Sor-Juana-Ines-de-la-Cruz

July Westhale is a novelist, translator, and the award-winning author of six books, including *Via Negativa*, which Publishers Weekly called "stunning" in a starred review. July's most recent work can be found in *McSweeney's*, *The National Poetry Review*, *Prairie Schooner*, *CALYX*, and *The Huffington Post*, among others. July is represented by Carolyn Forde at Transatlantic. www.julywesthale.co

Advance Praise

Unmade Hearts defies description as a "poetry collection"—better yet, it moves the benchmark of what poetry can be toward a glittering, heretofore un-glimpsed horizon. Through scorching honesty, playful wit, and the aching beauty of absolute, emotional communion—two souls performing mental yoga poses, stretched to the utmost inward toward memory and outward toward one another, simultaneously—July Westhale's translations and marginal notes on Sor Juana Inés de la Cruz's sonnets conjure a brilliant dialogue across desires, languages, and centuries. This is essential reading for poets, translators, and everyone who has ever tried-succeeded-failed-hoped to love and be loved.

Pamela Petro, author of *The Long Field*

What better way to introduce, or reintroduce, yourself to the lyrical divine that is Sor Juana Inés de la Cruz than to see "this 17th century Mexican nun rly sliding into [Westhale's] DMs"? *Unmade Hearts* is not only a brilliantly textured and careful translation of Sor Juana's work, but it reads like love letters between Sor Juana and Westhale across centuries. These time-traveling pen pals are in conversation about love, about the Divine, and if there really is a difference between the two. Westhale expertly uses white space to give these fragments alternating breathing room and urgency. Westhale's translation notes from the margins serve to break the fourth wall and welcome the reader into the passionate back and forth. Go and dig into this delicious reworking of Sor Juana!

Boston Gordon, author of *Glory Holes*

Reading this collection, 17th century nun Sor Juana feels suspended, as if caught in amber. It takes the skill and prowess of someone like poet and translator July Westhale, with her intellectual chops, to crack Sor Juana out of this suspension. This freeing results in the immediacy of Sor Juana's living voice and presence on the page. As a conversation, questions arise about love, suffering, spirituality, sexuality, and identity, a resinous amalgamation which kept me stuck, caught in the text, reading the whole book in one sitting.

Rev. Susan Baller-Shepard, author of *Doe*

About Small Harbor Publishing

Small Harbor Publishing is a 501c3 nonprofit organization. Our goal is to publish unique and diverse voices. We are a feminist press, and we are committed to diversity and inclusion. We strive to bring new voices to a devoted and expanding readership.

Small Harbor Publishing began in 2018 with the first issue of *Harbor Review*. The magazine is an online space where poetry and art converse. *Harbor Review* quickly grew and now publishes reviews and runs multiple micro chapbook competitions, including the Washburn Prize and the Editor's Prize.

In July 2020, Small Harbor Publishing was officially incorporated and began Harbor Editions. Harbor Editions accepts submissions through a chapbook open reading period, a hybrid chapbook open reading period, the Marginalia Series, and the Laureate Prize.

In 2023, Harbor Anthologies began with a mission to promote texts that explore social justice issues and highlight marginalized writers.

If you would like to support Small Harbor Publishing, please visit our "About" page at smallharborpublishing.com/about.

www.ingramcontent.com/pod-product-compliance
Lightning Source LLC
Chambersburg PA
CBHW020215090426
42734CB00008B/1087